WhatsApp Messenger:
Timeline, Features, and
Usages in Christian
Ministries

Adebayo Afolaranmi

ISBN: 978-1-79478-261-7

Published by

Lulu Press, Inc.   lulu
3101 Hillsborough Street
Raleigh, NC 27607
United States of America

Contents

Introduction

Since the advent of the Internet some decades ago, and the evolution of social media in general and instant messaging apps or platforms in particular, there has been no form of online communication accepted and widely used as WhatsApp Messenger. It has taken over from many other instant messaging apps that used to be in vogue like Yahoo Messenger and BlackBerry Messenger, and many others that are still in operation presently like Telegram Messenger, Imo Messenger and the likes are just competing with it, they have not been able to match its acceptance and usage. Billions of people throughout the world are now making use of WhatsApp for communication and other purposes.

This booklet gives brief history and milestone of WhatsApp Messanger since its inception, some of the major features of the app, some cautions one has to make in using the app, and how the app can be used effectively in Christians ministries. This

last part is majorly out my personal experiences of using the app since around 2012.
God bless you!

Adebayo Ola Afolaranmi
+2348055159591
spiritualdigest@yahoo.com
November 27, 2019

Origin and Timeline

Whatsapp Messenger is a cross-platform mobile messaging app that allows one to exchange messages, images, audio or video without having to pay for SMS but using the Internet. WhatsApp Messenger is available for iPhone, BlackBerry, Android, Windows Phone and Nokia. It can also be used on computer by simply going to the Whatsapp website and download it to Mac or Windows. It is becoming the most popular instant message (IM) app.

A brief timeline of this app will be helpful here:

✓ **Brian Acton** and **Jan Koum**, who used to be employees of Yahoo!, founded WhatsApp in 2009 (to be precise February 24, 2009 when it was incorporates WhatsApp in California).

✓ WhatsApp 2.0 was released on the App Store for the iPhone in August 2009, and by December that year, WhatsApp for the iPhone is updated to send photos.

✓ By August 2012, WhatsApp messages were **encrypted** in the "latest version" of the WhatsApp software for iOS and Android.

✓ WhatsApp's user base swelled to about 200 million active users by February 2013.

✓ By July 16, 2013 WhatsApp became **free**.

- ✓ WhatsApp introduced **voice messaging** in August 2013.
- ✓ On February 19, 2014, **Facebook** announces its acquisition of WhatsApp for US$19 billion.
- ✓ In November 2014, WhatsApp introduced a feature named **"Read Receipts"** that alerts senders when their messages are read by recipients. Within a week, WhatsApp introduced an update allowing users to disable this feature so that message recipients do not send acknowledgements.
- ✓ On January 21, 2015, WhatsApp launched **WhatsApp Web**, a web client that can be used through a web browser by syncing with the mobile device's connection.
- ✓ On the same day, WhatsApp announced its policy on cracking down on 3rd-party clients, including WhatsApp+. By this, users would not be able to use WhatsApp's services at all until the third-party apps are uninstalled.
- ✓ On January 18, 2016, WhatsApp's co-founder, Jan Koum, announced that WhatsApp will no longer charge its users a $1 annual subscription fee in an effort to

remove a barrier faced by users without credit cards, although, there was still no clear plan for monetizing WhatsApp.

- ✓ On March 2, 2016, WhatsApp introduced its **document-sharing** feature, initially allowing users to share PDF files with their contacts.
- ✓ WhatsApp is introduced for both Windows and Mac operating systems on May 10, 2016.
- ✓ On November 10, 2016, WhatsApp launched a beta version of **two-step verification** for Android users, which allowed them to use their email addresses for further protection.
- ✓ WhatsApp started external testing of an enterprise platform that enables companies to provide customer service to users at scale on September 5, 2017.
- ✓ In January 2018, WhatsApp launched **WhatsApp Business** for small business use.
- ✓ Later in September 2018, WhatsApp introduced **group audio and video call** features.

- ✓ In October, the **"Swipe to Reply"** option was added to the Android beta version, 16 months after it was introduced for iOS.
- ✓ In November 2019, WhatsApp released a new privacy feature that let users decide who adds them to the group.

Features

Some of the features of WhatsApp have been mentioned above as it evolves. The popularity of the free messaging app has got its developers to keep upgrading more and more features on WhatsApp. So, some of these features will still be highlighted below:

Sending and Receiving Text Messages
One can send and receive text messages through WhatsApp without being charged any amount as in sending SMS provided one is online. This is the most valuable feature of WhatsApp, and most of the other features hang on it. The same message can be sent to multiple people without these people knowing. Previously, WhatsApp users could send or forward a message to 20 people and/groups at a time. However, to guard against fake news and scams, one can only send or forward a message to 20 people and/groups at a time.

Profile Name, Picture and Status
If one has a WhatsApp Messenger account, one will certainly have a profile with a name that one uses to probably open the account apart from one's phone number, and possibly profile picture and profile status. The default WhatsApp status is "Hey there! I am using WhatsApp". Other

default statuses provided by WhatsApp are: "Available", "Busy", "Urgent Calls Only", "Can't talk, WhatsApp Only", and the likes.

Status Message
One can send a message and/or picture as status message in WhatsApp Messenger. This message and/or picture will be visible to one's contacts for 24 hours only. One's contacts can respond to the message and/or picture by swiping up the message and/or picture and type something as a reply.

Group Chat
One can keep in touch with groups of people that matter the most, like one's family or coworkers. With group chats, one can share messages, photos, and videos with up to 256 people at once. One can also name one's group, mute or customize notifications, and more. WhatsApp groups can be open ones where every group member can post or reply to a post, or close ones where only group administrator(s) or admin(s) can post or reply to a post. One can change the status of group from open to close at any time. Each group can have a group name, picture, and description that can be changed at any time also. Each group also has a unique web link that anyone can use to access and possibly join the group. Furthermore, group creators can dismiss

group admins using the "Dismiss As Admin" option. The creators can also restrict admins from changing group icon, subject or description.

Permission of Adding to Groups/Group Blocking
One now has control over who can add one to his or her group. One will be able to choose people by whom one or they do not want to join a group. If one activates this feature, people will be blocked from placing one in a group chat without getting one's permission first. To activate this, one should be sure that one has update to the latest version of WhatsApp on one's phone. Then one should follow these steps: Open the WhatsApp app. Go to Settings, to Account, to Privacy. Tap on Groups. From here, one can choose one of three available options. Picking 'Everyone' will let anyone add one to a group without asking one for permission. Choosing 'My Contacts' will limit group-adding to people in one's phone contacts – forcing everyone else to invite one first. And choosing 'Nobody' will require everyone to ask for one's permission before one can be added to a group.

Broadcast Lists
WhatsApp provides avenue for one to create broadcast lists of at 256 people. For these people to be able to receive a message sent through broadcast lists, they must have one's contacts on

their phone contact lists. The advantage of this is that only the creator of the list can send through the list. To create a broadcast list, simply click on the menu (three dot ellipse) and select 'New broadcast'. Click on the '+' sign on the right and select the names from one's contact list. The difference between broadcast message and group message is that only the sender will receive any response to the broadcast message as individual chat while all the group members will get any response to a sent message (if the group is an open one).

Forwarding Restrictions and Labelled Forwarded Messages
To tackle the spread of fake news and bogus messages on the platform, WhatsApp has put up strict restrictions on message forwarding. Additionally, the app has started showing a "Forwarded" label next of any messages that have been forwarded by other users.

Voice and Video Calls
One can make voice or/and video calls through WhatsApp. It is just like making ordinary calls. Just select the contact of person one wants to call and place the call. One can select if one wants the call to be mere voice or audio call or video call where both of you will be able to see live video of each other as one makes the call.

Group Video and Voice Calling
One can make group calling by adding participants to a call. The WhatsApp group calling currently supports just up to four people.

Sending Long Duration Audio Recordings
One can press and hold the microphone icon and then slide it to a lock button. By this, one can record long messages hands-free.

Hearing Voice Messages Privately Via Earpiece
One can hear voice messages that one receives on WhatsApp using one's phone's earpiece (one that one uses to hear other persons voice during phone calls). To do this, one can play a WhatsApp voice recorded message, and lift the phone to one's ear – the same way that one would attend a phone call – and the message will automatically start playing via the earpiece.

WhatsApp Web
On January 21, 2015, WhatsApp was officially made available for PCs through a web client, under the name **WhatsApp Web** – a browser-based web client that could be used by syncing with a mobile device's connection. To use this, one has to go to **www.web.whatsapp.com** on one's computer and scan the QR code shown there. Once the code is scanned through one's

device, the WhatsApp account on the laptop will be opened. The WhatsApp user's handset must still be connected to the Internet for the browser application to function. With WhatsApp on the web and desktop, one can seamlessly sync all of one's chats to one's computer so that one can chat on whatever device is most convenient for one. This has made transfer of files between one's phone and computer possible.

Security by Default (End-to-End Encryption)
This makes messages, photos, videos, voice messages, voice messages, documents, status updates and calls to be secured from falling into wrong hands by ensuring that only the sender and the intended receiver can access what is sent.

Photos and Videos
WhatsApp has made sending of photos, images, and videos easy. One can even take the picture and send it instantly to other people through WhatsApp.

Sending and Receiving Documents
One can send and receive PDFs, documents, spreadsheets, slideshows and more, without the hassle of email or file sharing apps. One can send documents up to 100 MB. Sharing of contact details as one has them on the contact list of one's phone is now very easy through WhatsApp.

Documents can be directly shared from one's Google Drive and iCloud Drive into a WhatsApp chat through this feature.

Voice Messages
With just one tap one can record a Voice Message, perfect for a quick hello or a longer story.

Formatting Text
One can now send messages in bold, italics or strikethrough too. Simply use the special characters before and after the words to get the formatting of one's choice. For example, use asterisk for **bold** (*hello*), underscore for *italics* (_hello_) and tilde for ~~strikethrough~~ (~hello~).

Frequent Chats
If one wants to know who one is chatting too much with on WhatsApp, one can find out by simply scrolling through the chat screen. However, if one has cleared out the messages or if they are too many, it will be difficult to find out easily. For this, one can go to the settings and click on 'Settings', then 'Account' and then 'Storage Usage'. Here one will find a list of contacts one is presently chatting with and if one taps anyone, one can find out how much of data one has sent or received during all chats. Now one can probably find out who is one's good pal.

Unfortunately, this feature is available only on iPhone for now.

Saving Data on Mobile Networks and Stopping Auto Download
If one is roaming, or if one is on a slow or expensive data network, one can choose to reduce one's data consumption by selecting what one wants to automatically download. One can choose to selectively download video, photo or audio when one is roaming. Additionally, one can also click on 'Low data usage' to reduce the amount of data used during a WhatsApp call. To do this, one can go to "Settings", then go to "Data and storage usage", then select what one wants.

Muting Chats and Groups
If one is on a group that sends too many messages across or if one's friend sends too many unwanted messages, one can simply mute the group or contact to stop alerting one. One can choose to mute the audio alert or the notification respectively. The messages will come in but will only show when one starts WhatsApp. To activate this, select the contact or group and choose the 'mute' option from the menu.

Privacy Control
If one does not like to show anyone on one's contact list that one is using WhatsApp, one can

shut off the 'last seen' option from showing up on one's screen. One can also select to disable blue ticks (a form of read receipts) and turn off one's profile photo. To activate this, one can go to 'Settings' and find it in the 'Privacy' option. However, one should know that if one disables these options, one would not be able to see or read the same from other contacts too.

Reading Messages Without the Blue Ticks
When one reads a message, one is also sending back a read receipt to the sender. This way, the sender knows that one has seen the message. However, if one does not want to send a read receipt (blue tick) back to the sender, one can read the message without the sender knowing it with two simple tricks. If one wants to read a message, one should simply cut off all data networks to one's phone. Then, one should use airplane mode and turn off Wi-Fi. Then, one should open WhatsApp, read the message. Once done, one should close WhatsApp by killing it from the memory too (use an app killer if needed) and then start one's data again. This may seem tedious. The other simpler trick is to add a WhatsApp Widget on one's desktop. If a message arrives, one can read the entire message without the sender knowing it by simply scroll the message on the Widget. However, one should

beware because if one clicks on the widget, one will trigger
WhatsApp and a blue tick will be sent across.

Adding Shortcuts to One's Home Screen (or Desktop) for Individual Chats
If one is constantly chatting with a few friends, or some important contacts, one can reduce the time to start WhatsApp and hunt for the name of the person(s) and start a conversation. One can simply long press on the contact and select 'Add chat shortcut' from the menu. One can add the chat contact directly to one's desktop and start chatting from there itself.

Sending Messages to Oneself
Sometimes one needs to test a message before sending them out. One can send such messages to oneself on WhatsApp before sending it to other people. To do this, one should simply create a WhatsApp group, add a friend and then delete him from the group. Now one is alone in that group, and one can send messages there. It is also a great option for taking quick notes!

Protecting One's Chats by Disabling Notification Preview
Even if WhatsApp is not opened, one can see that message scroll in one's notification bar when one receives a message. Though this feature, one

could have sensitive messages being read by undesirable people glancing into one's phone. To avoid this, one should simply head to the phone's settings and disable notifications for WhatsApp. Once done, WhatsApp will not show anything on the notification bar.

Sending and Receiving Emoticons
The word emoticon is derived from two words: emotions and icons. Emoticons are a shorthand method of explaining a feeling like smiles, frowns, winks, and the likes on the Internet. They grew from clever combinations of punctuation marks that now are usually translated by software into an actual face. To use this feature on WhatsApp, one can press the key showing an emoticon of face as one is typing one's message, and more emoticons will surface to be used.

Whatsapp Sticker Packs
WhatsApp has also added a rich collection of expressive stickers next to Smileys and GIF options. One can download different sticker packs, rearrange them, add personal ones and even use third-party apps like 'Personal Stickers for WhatsApp' to further customize them.

Quoting Messages Within Chats
One can quote a particular message and reply accordingly. If one is in a huge WhatsApp group

or in a long conversation with someone, one can refer to a particular message that one is replying with quotes by simply longing press on the particular message in the list and one will see the reply option popup. By clicking on reply, one's quoted message will appear as a box along with one's reply.

Blocking Unwanted People and Spam
When one receives messages from unknown contacts or simply spam messages with advertisements and promotions, one can simply cut them off from repeatedly coming to one's phone by marking them as spam. To do this, one can open the unknown message and one will find two options 'add to contacts' and 'spam'. One should choose accordingly.

Calling or Sending Message by WhatsApp through Phone Contact List
One can initiate a call or send message by WhatsApp through one's phone contact list or address book. This can be done by opening one's phone contact list and look for the contact that one wants to call or sends a message to. If the person is on WhatsApp, the WhatsApp icon will show with the contact's details, and clicking on that icon will lead one automatically to WhatsApp app and initiate the call or open the

message box for one to type and send the message.

Deleting Multiple Chats
To delete multiple messages from one's chat list, simply long press on a single chat or message and continue tapping on multiple ones after that, then delete them from the options menu.

Star Messages
One can highlight some messages and store them as favourites. These are called 'star' messages in WhatsApp. To do this, long press on the message in the chat and click on the star icon. These messages will be saved as favourites within the chat itself. And if one wishes to delete the chat, one can also have the option to keep the starred messages and delete the rest.

Marking as Unread Message
One can mark chats as unread so that they can be read later. There are times when one wants to read the entire message from the contact or group, but due to shortage of time, one may prefer to read it later. However, one could forget about it too. So, one can mark them as unread to read it up later. One can also mark chats as unread to mark them as important for later too. To mark message as unread, long press on the chat and select as unread from the options menu.

Direct Reply from Notification Bar

If one receives a message on WhatsApp, one can see it in the notification bar (if one has turned this off). One can directly reply back without opening WhatsApp by pulling down the notification bar and hitting 'reply' to instantly reply to that message thereby avoiding wasting time opening WhatsApp.

Backup to Google Drive

One can save one's entire chats and files from WhatsApp by backing them up to one's Google Drive. This can help one in case one changes one's smartphone, or lose it. One can restore one's data back to one's WhatsApp in case one switches to another phone. To do this, from the settings, one can choose backup and then choose to backup to Google Drive. One should then follow the procedure on the screen to allow Google to access one's WhatsApp. One can also choose to backup only chats or media and documents too. However, backing up to Google drive will cost one online space and data bandwidth.

Backup/Exporting Chats and Media to Email

Backup or export particular chats for safekeeping in email. In the chat screen, click on the 'options' menu, then 'more' and then on 'email chat'. One can send the entire chat with or without the media elements to one's desired email address in this process.

Change of Wallpaper
One can choose to give one's chat screen a different look compared with the stock WhatsApp background. To do this, one can choose from the wallpaper of one's choice from 'options – chats – wallpaper'. One can even use one's picture instead of wallpaper here!

Using Different Languages
If one desires, one can type and send messages in the language of one's choice from the available languages. To do this, one can go to 'options', then 'chats' and then 'app language'.

Searching Messages
One can search for particular message within long chats. If one is part of a large WhatsApp group, or if one is chatting with a contact for a long time, finding a particular message may become a task. One could either mark important messages with a star or simply use the search feature to hunt for a particular message. To find a message, one can click on the 'search' icon on the top and enter the text for one's search.

Auto Answering WhatsApp Messages
If one uses WhatsApp for professional reasons and wishes to add an automatic reply message to WhatsApp conversations, there are several apps one can use to achieve that. One app that one can try is "Auto Reply for WhatsApp".

Getting Early Updates
To get the latest features on WhatsApp, one has to wait for the public release of WhatsApp for them. However, if one is a beta user, one can get early releases before it is publically released on the app market. To become a beta user, register for it online, and henceforth one will receive daily updates with bug fixes, patches and new features before it is even released to be public. These beta versions are for beta testers and becoming a beta tester is free.

Knowing Who Has Read One's Messages in a Group
If one is sending messages to a large group, it will be difficult to know who has read one's message and who has not. When one sends a message, one will see a single tick. When one sees a double tick, it means that everyone in the group has received one's message. When the tick turns blue, it means that all the group members have read the message. However, if one only sees a double grey tick and want to know who all have one's

message, one should simply long press on the sent message and click the 'i' (information) button on the top. This option will tell one how many people have received the message, how many have yet to receive it and how many have read it. On a single one-to-one chat, one can use this option to find out when the recipient read it with date and time information.

Sending One's Location with Maps
If one is meeting a friend, or want to send one's friend to a particular location/address or simply want to invite someone to where one is, one can send a Google Map location on WhatsApp. All one needs to do is enable GPS, then tap on the attachment icon (the paperclip icon) and choose location. Google Maps will open up, and one can simply mark the location pin and send it on WhatsApp. The recipient can then click in the message, open Maps and follow the map to reach the destination.

Sharing Live Location
One can share live location with one's contacts. The location is updated in real-time and one can keep a tab on exact whereabouts of specific contacts. One can share location for 15 minutes, 1 hour or 8 hours straight. To do this, one can tap the attachment icon in the text input field, then

select 'location' and then select 'Share Live Location'.

Pulling Back One's Accidentally Sent Messages
One can pull back one's messages if one has accidentally sent them to the recipient. The message could be incomplete or unwanted. When message is sent and one wants to pull it back, one has to quickly hit the airplane mode. If one's data connection is fast, one could be late. However, if one's Internet connection is a little slower, one can halt the message before it heads outwards. Hitting the airplane mode could cut off the Internet connection, and one's message will not get through. At the moment, one can delete the message and turn on data back again. This has to be really done quickly! If the message is not up to 60 minutes, one can delete or "unsend" the sent message. To do this, one should long press the message and select delete for everyone.

Reading Deleted Messages on WhatsApp
There is a way to read messages that one's friends have deleted from their end. One can download a "notification log app" and grant access to read the notification. This app will keep a log of all incoming notifications and will also come in handy when one wishes to retrieve a notification that one has accidentally swiped off.

Delete Images or Videos from a Particular Whatsapp Group or Contact

If a particular WhatsApp group or contact is dominating storage space, one can delete messages, chats, videos, and audio from a specific WhatsApp group. To do this one can go to Settings, then 'Data and Storage usage', and then select 'Storage Usage' and one will see all groups and contacts ranked according to the storage space they are keeping. One should then select the group and tap on the 'manage messages' option at the bottom, then select and clear whatever data (videos, GIFs, Photos, etc.) one wishes to get rid of.

Transferring WhatsApp from Old Phone to New One

Transferring WhatsApp from old phone to new one could be a little tedious compared to apps like Gmail, Facebook, Games, etc. that have their data stored online and not on the phone. There are two methods for for doing this. One is to use the feature within the app itself by backing up one's WhatsApp online with Google drive, installing WhatsApp on one's new phone and activating it. WhatsApp will sense that one has some data online and will ask if one wants to restore it. The second method is to use a desktop PC and transfer the entire WhatsApp folder from the internal storage of the old phone to the new phone. One should install WhatsApp on the new phone and activate it only after one has transferred the folder to the same location on the new phone. WhatsApp will sense that one has some data on the phone and will ask if one wants to import it.

Changing WhatsApp Number
If one is discontinuing the number registered with WhatsApp, one can replace it with one's new number and keep using the same WhatsApp account. One can do this by finding the option under Settings, then Account, then Change Number. One's new number should be active to do so.

Hiding Whatsapp Group Photos and Videos from Gallery
Since most of us do not have much control over what content is pushed to our phones via WhatsApp groups, and this content showing up in our phone's gallery can be a huge problem, WhatsApp has now added the option to hide media from particular groups in the gallery. To do this, open a WhatsApp group and tap on the group name to access the option. This method will not remove already existing WhatsApp images in one's gallery. One will have to delete them. The new incoming media will be hidden.

Hiding Particular Contacts from Viewing One's Story or Updates

If one does not want to share stories with all WhatsApp contacts, one can prohibit particular contacts from viewing one's status updates or stories. To do this, one can go to WhatsApp settings, then Account, then Privacy. One should select Status, then 'My contacts except'. One should then select specific contacts one wishes to avoid and tap the tick mark below. One can also select the "Only share with" option if one wishes to share status updates only with a small number of specific contacts.

Fingerprint Lock

One could reply from the notification shade and answer calls on WhatsApp when the app is locked.

Schedule of WhatsApp Messages

To schedule WhatsApp messages for groups or individual contacts, one can download the "Scheduler app for WhatsApp". After granting it Accessibility permission, one can fill in the required fields and schedule one's message.

Assign Different Priority and Sound to Different Notifications

WhatsApp has added support for 'Notification Channels' to set priority for different types of notifications coming from the same app. So, one can decide if one needs group messages to pop up or not. One can also assign them a priority level to determine how often they make it to the notification panel. To use this feature, one can long press app notifications and then select the manage notification option.

Pinning Conversation or Making Shortcuts
If one wishes to keep a particular contact or conversation on top, one can long press the conversation and select the Pin icon in the options menu that appears on top. One can also press the triple dot menu and select create shortcut option to place the conservation shortcut on the main page.

Hiding a WhatsApp Chat
People whom one has recently talked to appear closer to the top in one's WhatsApp chat list. If one does not want a particular conversation to be noticeable, one can hide it as "Archive". To do this one can long press the conversation and select the Archive button on the top. This particular chat will disappear from the list. One can access it by scrolling all the way to the bottom.

Setting Up Reminders
This is a new feature. Users that want to set up reminders will need to download a separate app called "Any.do" after WhatsApp announced a partnership with them. Once the two apps are linked, users can create and receive reminders within the messaging platform. Sending texts like "Remind me to check the mailbox on my way home" will prompt a response confirming the reminder. Once the time comes, Any.do will send the user a Whatsapp message to remind them. For now, to access this feature, users must download a premium account costing about £5 a month.

WhatsApp Call Waiting
If one uses WhatsApp to make a lot of phone calls, one might have probably been in the situation where one is on the phone with someone and another contact tries to call one. Previously, WhatsApp would not alert one if someone else was trying to reach one at the same time. Instead, one would have to wait until one got off the phone to see one had missed a call. In a recent WhatsApp update for iPhone and Android, call waiting has been added. That means if one is on the phone with a contact and someone else tries to call one, a notification will appear at the top of one's device. This will allow

one to decline the second caller or end one's current call and accept the newest one.

WhatsApp Business API
MessageBird hosts this feature and it is not free to use. MessageBird's WhatsApp Business allows one to connect to one's customers on the world's most popular messaging app via MessageBird's API, Flow Builder low-code solution, or native Zendesk integration. Through it, one can send and receive WhatsApp messages for customer support, alerts and notifications, as well as two-factor authentication. MessageBird's Whatsapp Business API offers one the following benefits: easy integration, speed and deliverability, end-to-end WhatsApp encryption, rich messaging, and 24/7 supports. Since it is mainly for business, to operate it, each business account must apply to WhatsApp for approval before gaining access to the WhatsApp Business API. One can simply follow the step-by-step WhatsApp onboarding quickstart of MessageBird, and they will walk one through the approval process, choosing a WhatsApp number, connecting WhatsApp to one's MessageBird Account, installing WhatsApp, and more.

Usages of WhatsApp in Christian Ministries

By being the most popular instant message (IM) app today with tens of features as underscored above, WhatsApp has become a veritable tool in Christian ministries. Here some of the ways one can make use of WhatsApp in Christian ministries. Since some of these uses have been explained under the features above, how to apply them in ministering to others will be explained here. The applications here are not exhaustive. As one is getting familiar with, and using each of the features of WhatsApp, one will be discovering how peculiarly apply them in one's Christian ministries.

Profile Name
One can decide to use one's real name, nickname, name of ministry/church, combination of characters, or even smiley, website address, and so on as profile name. There is even an opportunity to use a short profile as one's display name. Undoubtedly, this will give one's contacts or anyone that sees one's profile name in one's contacts' lists or a group a message about one.

Profile Picture
Apart from one's picture or other desired picture, one can use a designed logo or poster about one's

ministry/church or a religious event that is about to take place, or just a poster with a specific message like Bible verse(s) or inspiring quote, as one's profile picture. People that have one in their contacts' lists and/or belong to same group(s) with one will see the profile picture/poster and may tend to read the message in the profile picture/poster. One can use a desired picture, logo or poster as displayed picture for group chats also.

Profile Status
Instead of using any of the WhatsApp default statuses, one can use a customised status of at most 140 characters that may be a short inspiring quote, a short Bible verse, short information about one's ministry/church or a religious event. People that have one in their contacts' lists and/or belong to same group(s) with one will see the profile status and may tend to read the message.

Individual Chat
As one can chat individually with any person in one's WhatsApp contact list. Apart from sending devotional messages, sermons, Bible study outlines, short quotes, prayer wishes, and so on through this individual chatting. This is good especially for counselling and praying with/for individuals in one's WhatsApp contact list.

Status Message
One can send a picture and/or message in form of short quotes, prayer wishes, and so on as status message that will be visible to one's contacts for 24 hours only.

Group Chat/Messages
As there is opportunity of creating WhatsApp groups or joining existing ones, one can use these groups to send devotional messages, sermons, Bible study outlines, short quotes, prayer wishes, and so on to members of these groups, and if the group is an open one, each of the group members can respond to the sent messages. If the group is an open one, members can engage one another in discussion about the issues in the Bible and other edifying issues.

Broadcast Messages
Devotional messages, sermons, Bible study outlines, short quotes, prayer wishes, and so on can be sent as many times as possible through broadcast lists. A message received through either individual chat, group chat or broadcast message can be sent or forwarded to other people through one's individual chat, group chat or broadcast message.

Voice and Video Calls

Voice or/and video calls through WhatsApp can be used to send information and to minister to people, especially praying for, and counseling other people. With WhatsApp group calling, one can hold a sort of conference, service, prayer session, and the like through WhatsApp.

Sending Documents/Images
One can send documents or images like files, pictures, logos or posters with messages about one's church/ministry. Recorded messages and audio/video messages or events can be sent easily through WhatsApp.

Sending and Receiving Emoticons and Sticker Packs
Emoticons, "stickers" and "emojis" can be used as expressions when one is chatting with, and especially counseling, other people.

Knowing Who Has Read One's Messages in a Group
This feature is a source of motivation as one is able to know the impact of one's message on the group members, especially knowing those that have/have not read one's message in the group. It is a way of monitoring group members also. One can appreciate those that are frequently reading one's messages, and one can rebuke or encourage those that are not reading the messages.

Sending or Sharing Location
One can send or share the location of one's church or where an event will take place with one's contacts.

Pulling Back One's Accidentally Sent Messages
If one has accidentally sent a message to one's contacts or a group, one can pull back the message thereby saving one from the embarrassment that such message may cause one's reputation and ministry.

Schedule of WhatsApp Messages and Setting Up Reminders
In a situation where one is very busy with ministry activities, one can schedule messages to be sent later. This is good especially for birthdays, anniversaries, and other important days that one ought not to forget. Using WhatsApp scheduling feature will help in delivering the desired message at the desired time.

Disadvantages and Limitations of WhatsApp Messenger

As good as WhatsApp Messenger is, the instant messaging app have some disadvantages and limitations. Among them are:

- Only smartphones are supported, and many people still do not have them. Besides, WhatsApp only works on phones that are packet-data enabled or Wi-Fi enabled.
- A user cannot send or receive messages without being online.
- The WhatsApp messenger group has only limitation to add 256 people.
- Storing or Retrieving the Chats Backup can be very messy sometimes.
- Constant group messages are unavoidable, and these can take up maximum space. This takes much time to empty the WhatsApp space.
- There is risk because any close person may read the messages on WhatsApp.
- One's profile picture is visible to every person having one's contact number.
- One cannot send a message to more than 5 people or/and groups at a time.

- Unlike Telegram and Facebook, messages already sent on WhatsApp cannot be edited.
- WhatsApp has been proven unsecure due to the frequent hack as WhatsApp also faces spam-problems.
- There is limited status sharing as only 140 characters are allowed.
- Status message sharing with contacts are visible for only 24 hours.
- After deleting a message, the people one sent it to will know that one deleted it. This is quite terrible unlike Telegram where people will not know that one has deleted a message.
- The captions along with pictures and videos cannot be forwarded, however it shows 'selected' while forwarding. It causes a lot of misunderstanding and chaos.
- 'Share with Whatsapp' button is mostly not available with most webpages, while one can share it with Facebook or Twitter.
- An unused/left account will be active without any verification when another user owns the same mobile number. So one's

information can be shared with an unknown person.

➢ No search option to find a new contact that is not available in one's contact list (as in Skype).

➢ Voice call is not supported in some countries.

➢ Typing is a trouble for long text messages, though this can be overcome by using a PC or laptop for WhatsApp Web.

➢ The desktop version (WhatsApp Web) is not truly independent. One needs one's smartphone around to read the QR code and both the phone and the computer must be connected with the Internet.

➢ WhatsApp is addictive. Once one gets addicted to it, it is very difficult to get over WhatsApp addiction.

➢ WhatsApp drains Smartphone batteries easily

➢ With WhatsApp, one's profile-picture is actually visible to anyone having one's contact number and available on WhatsApp whether one knows such person or not.

➢ WhatsApp can be distracting. In fact, it can easily disrupt employees at the workplace.

➢ One can be added to groups that one does not want to be a part of.
➢ Unlike BBM, people have to share their mobile numbers with one another in order to communicate.
➢ WhatsApp requires frequent upgrades that can be very disturbing.
➢ With WhatsApp, people can actually chat or make calls without meeting physically and this has actually made people unsocial today than never before.
➢ WhatsApp does not actually have a sign-out-option and this actually makes it very vulnerable to use especially for couples that like checking each other's phones.

Cautions

Recently, hackers started hacking WhatsApp Accounts by exploit people on group chats and give them fake news. The hackers will change one's phone number to theirs and replace the person in whatsoever group the person belongs. In order to prevent such a thing from happening, one should follow these steps to protect one's WhatsApp account:

> ➤ Go to settings on one's WhatsApp.
> ➤ Click on Account.
> ➤ Click on Two- step verification.
> ➤ Enter one's desired six-figure PIN that one will remember.
> ➤ Input one's email address.
> ➤ And save.

That is all! If someone wants to change it, WhatsApp will ask for the Two-step verification and without it the account will not open. Periodically, WhatsApp will be asking one also one's PIN. If one forgets, then one will be asked to perform the Two-step verification.

Conclusion

The rate at which WhatsApp Messenger is getting acceptability as a means of communication is alarming. The Lord has made it as a means to make communication gathering and dissemination easier than before. Christians should be ready to know the evolving features of this instant messaging app, and use them as veritable tools in the Christian ministries.

For Further Readings

"11 Hidden WhatsApp Features". Retrieved on November 25, 2019 from https://www.cnet.com/how-to/hidden-whatsapp-features/.

"30 Latest WhatsApp Hidden Features, Tips, and Tricks To Know In 2019". Retrieved on November 25, 2019 from https://www.smartprix.com/bytes/new-whatsapp-tips-and-tricks/.

"All of 40 WhatsApp features, tips and tricks you should know". Retrieved on November 25, 2019 from https://www.deccanchronicle.com/technology/mobiles-and-tabs/210616/40-whatsapp-tips-and-tricks-for-beginners-become-a-chat-jockey.html.

"Explainer: What is WhatsApp". Retrieved on November 25, 2019 from https://www.webwise.ie/parents/explainer-whatsapp/.

"Features." Retrieved on November 25, 2019 from https://www.whatsapp.com/features/.

"WhatsApp - Wikipedia." Retrieved on November 25, 2019 from https://en.wikipedia.org/wiki/WhatsApp.

"WhatsApp Messenger - Features, Tips, Advantages & Disadvantages". Retrieved on November 25, 2019 from https://www.informationq.com/whatsapp-messenger/.

"WhatsApp Messenger – Features, Tips, Advantages & Disadvantages." Retrieved on November 25, 2019 from https://www.informationq.com/whatsapp-messenger/.

"WhatsApp Update 2019". Retrieved on November 25, 2019 from https://www.messengerpeople.com/whatsapp-update-2019/.

"WhatsApp." Retrieved on November 25, 2019 from https://www.whatsacom/.

Afolaranmi, Adebayo Ola (2009). *Ministering through the Internet: An Essential Guide.* Ibadan: Charisa Books & Publishing.

WhatsApp User Manual: For front-line debt advisers using WhatsApp to support and communicate with clients. Manchester: Citizens Advice. Retrieved on November 25, 2019 from http://www.wiseradviser.org/uploads/general/WhatsApp_User_Manual_Final.pdf.

My Internet Ministry

"The Word through the Internet" (popularly known as **"Spiritual Digest"**) is an Internet ministry. Its goal is to REACH AS MANY PEOPLE AS POSSIBLE ALL OVER THE WORLD WITH THE WORD OF GOD THROUGH THE INTERNET.

The Word
Through
The Net

It is a ministry whereby **devotional messages are sent to people by email**. The first message was sent to about 50 people on February 18, 2003. Since then, the number of people that receive the messages every week has grown into thousands. Presently, these messages are sent in English and Esperanto languages once in a week mainly through web group services like Yahoo, MSN, AOL, Google, Facebook and others that offer free email group service on the Web. Apart from personal groups created in these services for sending the weekly messages to people, I belong to over four hundred other groups where I do send the messages to members of the groups. My main Yahoo groups in English are **Spiritual Digest Group** (http://groups.yahoo.com/group/spiritualdigest2003/) and **TheWordThrutheNet** Group (http://groups.yahoo.com/group/TheWor dThrutheNet/), and that of Esperanto is **SprirtaNutrajxo Esperanto Group** (http://groups.yahoo.com/group/spiritan utrajxo/). Also these weekly messages are sent to many Internet forums and weblogs. My main weblog is http://thewordthruthenet.blogspot.com/.

Another aspect of the ministry is **sending daily Bible verses and quotes with prayer/action for the day** from the Bible and other respected Christians and prayer wishes through WhatsApp Messenger, Facebook, Telegram Messenger and other social media and Yahoo group: http://groups.yahoo.com/group/spiritual digestdaily/. Visit this Facebook page: https://www.facebook.com/SpiritualDiges tfortheDay and click on the "Like" icon at its top so that you will be seeing these quotes and Bible verses every day on your Facebook homepage. A similar aspect is **Ministering through Daily Hymns** where you can receive daily-inspired hymns from me every day through this Facebook page: **https://www.facebook.com/Ministeri ngThroughDailyHymns**, WhatsApp Messenger and Telegram Messenger.

Furthermore, another aspect of the ministry is **sending of periodic inspiring**

50

quotes/prayer wishes to people by SMS. There is a **WEBLOG** (http://smspastorbayo.blogspot.com/) created for the collections of all these text messages (SMS) I have been sending to people. You can be part of this by sending your mobile phone number (including country code) to me.

Another aspect of the ministry is **sending of the Seek Daily devotions** (of the Nigerian Baptist Convention) through WhatsApp Messenger and Telegram Messenger.

Most of these aspects are now being done through **Facebook.com**. Join me at my **Facebook** (**www.facebook.com/afolabayo**) to be part of the ministry there.

Reactions of people to my messages have made me become a **prayer partner and counselor** to many people as they share their challenges with me. These have made me active online everyday as I respond to people's reactions, prayer requests and challenges by email, offline/online messages, SMS and BBM. At times, I engage in telephone conversations to do these.

GOD BLESS YOU!

You can order this
book and other books by me
online as
eBooks or printed books
from
http://www.lulu.com/spotlig
ht/spiritualdigest.
God bless you!

www.ingramcontent.com/pod-product-compliance
Lightning Source LLC
Chambersburg PA
CBHW070901070326
40690CB00009B/1944